Beginner's Guide to Crochet Cables

LEISURE ARTS, INC. • Maumelle, Arkansas

Items made and instructions tested by Marianna Crowder and Margaret Taverner.

ISBN-13: 978-1-4647-1266-1

Cables are not just for knitters anymore!

Crocheters have discovered an easy way to get the look using Post Stitches. These stitches add texture on top of the crocheted fabric because they are worked around the post of a stitch on a previous row. In this book, you'll learn how to combine and cross Post Stitches to create ropes and other cable patterns. Start with the cowl on page 6, and then build your skills with the next five projects. Camera icons 🎥 let you know when there are free online videos to help you learn the techniques.

Meet the Designer

Photo by Heather Weston

With more than 800 knit and crochet designs in print, Melissa Leapman is one of the most widely published American designers working today.

She began her design career by freelancing for leading ready-to-wear design houses in New York City, as well as working on commission for top yarn companies to create designs promoting their new and existing yarns each season. Her ability to quickly develop fully envisioned garments put her skills in great demand.

Through the years, Leisure Arts has published more than 40 books of Melissa's fabulous designs. Melissa is also the host of several Leisure Arts DVDs in the best-selling teach-yourself series, "I Can't Believe I'm Knitting" and "I Can't Believe I'm Crocheting."

Nationally, her designs have been featured in numerous magazines, and her workshops on knitting and crochet are consistently popular with crafters of all skill levels. She has taught at major events such as STITCHES, Vogue Knitting LIVE, and The Knitting Guild Association conferences, as well as at hundreds of yarn shops and local guild events across the country.

To find more of Melissa's exciting designs, visit LeisureArts.com, "like" Melissa's Facebook page, and join her group (Melissa Leapman Rocks) on Ravelry.com.

6

26

32

14

20

38

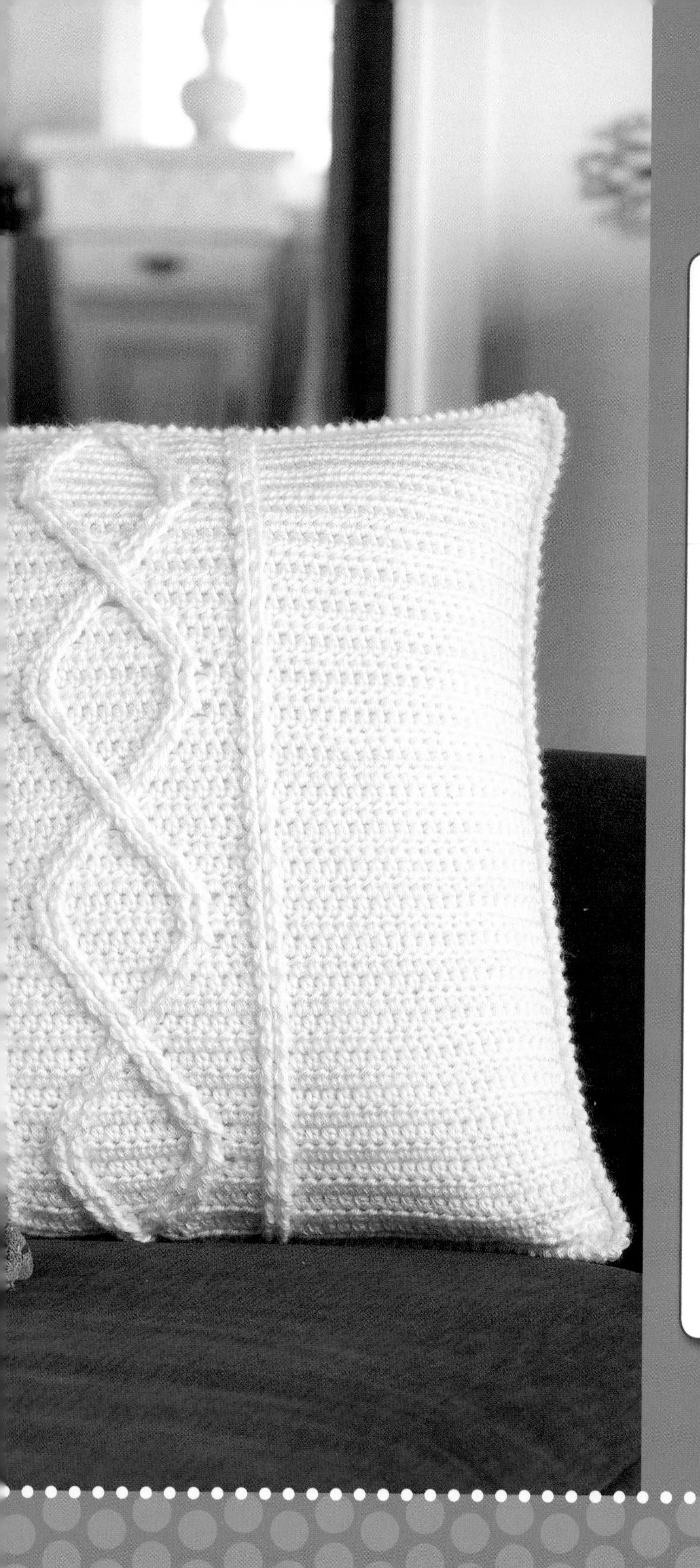

Beginner's Guide To Crochet Cables

While knitters have been creating cabled projects for a long time, crocheters have recently added this technique to their repertoire.

Cables are simply stitches worked out of sequence. Depending on how many stitches are involved, and whether they cross to the front or the back of others, creates the interesting texture.

Best of all, these intricate-looking fabrics are easy to make! Here's everything you need to know to crochet beautiful cables, including six projects with simple-to-follow instructions.

Happy Crocheting!

Getting Started

The easiest—and most fun—way to learn crocheted cables is to start with a simple project. In this book, the projects are arranged according to skill level. The first design, an infinity cowl, features textured rope cables. Begin with this pattern and work your way through the rest of the projects. Step by step, cable by cable, you'll soon be crocheting cables like a pro.

Supplies

To crochet cables, you'll only need basic supplies such as **medium weight yarn** and **crochet hooks**. Since stitch gauge is crucial to the success of the projects, a tape measure will come in handy. And, if the project requires seams, you'll need a large-eye tapestry or yarn needle.

Let's learn how to make a cable!

Rope Cable Infinity Cowl

EASY

Finished Measurement: 45" circumference x 12" wide (114.5 cm x 30.5 cm)

First, gather the supplies you will need!

SHOPPING LIST

Yarn (Medium Weight)

[3.5 ounces, 197 yards (100 grams, 180 meters) per skein]:

- ☐ 3 skeins

Crochet Hook

- ☐ Size J (6 mm) **or** size needed for gauge

Additional Supplies

- ☐ Yarn needle

Work the Gauge Swatch before you begin the Cowl.

GAUGE INFORMATION

In pattern, 12 sts and 9 rows = 4" (10 cm)

Gauge Swatch: 4" square (10 cm)

Ch 13.

Row 1: Hdc in third ch from hook **(2 skipped chs count as first hdc)** and in each ch across: 12 hdc.

Rows 2-9: Ch 2 **(counts as first hdc)**, hdc in next hdc and in each hdc across.

Finish off.

Now, you're ready to get started!

INSTRUCTIONS

Ch 37.

ROW 1

Hdc in back ridge of third ch from hook *(Fig. 4, page 46)* **(2 skipped chs count as first hdc)** and each ch across: 36 hdc.

ROW 2 (Right side)

Step 1 - Ch 2 **(counts as first hdc, now and throughout)**, turn; hdc in next 3 hdc.

Step 2 - YO twice *(Fig. A)*, insert hook from **front** to **back** around post of next hdc.

Fig. A

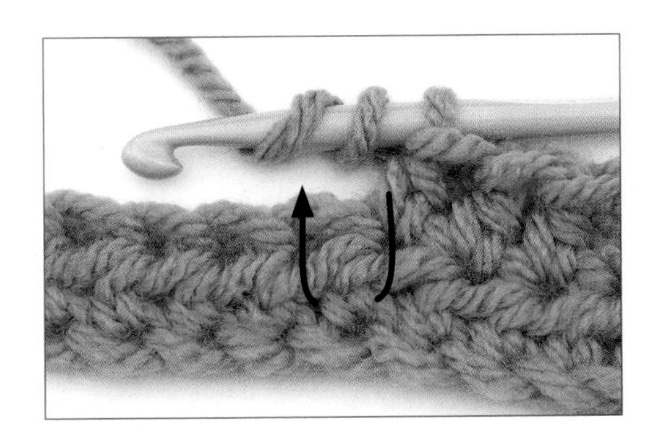

Step 3 - YO and pull up a loop (4 loops on hook) ***(Fig. B)***.

Fig. B

Step 4 - ★ YO and draw through 2 loops on hook; repeat from ★ 2 times **more (first FPtr made)** ***(Fig. C)***.

Fig. C

Repeat Steps 2-4, 3 times **more** *(Fig. D)*: 4 FPtr.

Fig. D

Look! You now have a group of 4-FPtr, which forms the beginning of a cable.

Step 5 - Hdc in next 4 hdc.

Repeat Steps 2-5, 3 times **more**: 20 hdc and 4 4-FPtr groups.

ROW 3

Ch 2, turn; hdc in next hdc and in each st across: 36 hdc.

The 4 FPdtr of the cable on Row 4 are worked around the 4-FPtr group in the row **below** the previous hdc row, skipping the 4 hdc **behind** it.

ROW 4

Step 1 - Ch 2, turn; hdc in next 3 hdc.

Step 2 - Skip next 2 FPtr one row **below**, YO 3 times *(Fig. E)*, insert hook from **front** to **back** around post of next FPtr.

Fig. E

Step 3 - YO and pull up a loop (5 loops on hook) *(Fig. F)*.

Fig. F

Step 4 - ★ YO and draw through 2 loops on hook; repeat from ★ 3 times **more (first FPdtr made)** *(Fig. G)*.

Fig. G

Look at the first FPdtr and see that it is leaning to the right. Now, let's make the second FPdtr.

Step 5 - YO 3 times, insert hook from **front** to **back** around post of next FPtr, YO and pull up a loop (5 loops on hook) *(Fig. H)*.

Fig. H

Step 6 - ★ YO and draw through 2 loops on hook; repeat from ★ 3 times **more (second FPdtr made)** *(Fig. I)*.

Fig. I

You have just completed the first half of the cable. Now let's finish the cable and make the last 2 FPdtr.

Step 7 - YO 3 times *(Fig. J)*, insert hook from **front** to **back** around first skipped FPtr.

Fig. J

Step 8 - YO and pull up a loop (5 loops on hook) *(Fig. K)*.

Fig. K

Step 9 - ★ YO and draw through 2 loops on hook; repeat from ★ 3 times **more (third FPdtr made)** *(Fig. L)*.

Fig. L

See how the third FPdtr is leaning to to the left on top of the first 2 FPdtr. Now, let's make the last FPdtr.

Step 10 - YO 3 times, insert hook from **front** to **back** around second skipped FPtr, YO and pull up a loop (5 loops on hook) *(Fig. M)*.

Fig. M

Step 11 - ★ YO and draw through 2 loops on hook; repeat from ★ 3 times **more (last FPdtr made)** *(Fig. N)*.

Fig. N

See how the first 2 FPdtr are leaning to the right under the last 2 FPdtr and the last 2 FPdtr are leaning to the left on top of the first 2 FPdtr. The 4 FPdtr have switched places.

Step 12 - Skip next 4 hdc from last hdc made, hdc in next 4 hdc *(Fig. O)*.

Fig. O

Repeat Steps 2-12, 3 times **more**: 20 hdc and 4 Cables.

Congratulations!

You have completed the first Cable row.
Now, you are ready to finish the Cowl.

ROW 5

Ch 2, turn; hdc in next hdc and in each st across: 36 hdc.

ROW 6

Ch 2, hdc in next 3 hdc, ★ work FPtr around each of next 4 FPdtr one row **below**, hdc in next 4 hdc; repeat from ★ 3 times **more**: 20 hdc and 4 4 FPtr groups.

Repeat Rows 3-6 until piece measures approximately 45" (114.5 cm) from beginning ch, ending by working Row 5.

Finish off, leaving a long end for sewing.

With **wrong** side together, fold piece in half, bringing short edges together. Thread yarn needle with long end and whipstitch short edges together *(Fig. 7, page 46)*.

What an accomplishment!

You've learned how to make
a basic 4 stitch cable.
Now, you're ready to go cable crazy
with any of the other designs!

Diamonds Throw Pillow

Finished SIze: 18" (45.5 cm) square

SHOPPING LIST

Yarn (Medium Weight) 

[6 ounces, 315 yards (170 grams, 288 meters) per skein**]**:

☐ 3 skeins

Crochet Hook

☐ Size H (5 mm) **or** size needed for gauge

Additional Supplies

☐ 18" (45.5 cm) square Pillow form

GAUGE INFORMATION

In pattern, 15 sts and 12 rows = 4" (10 cm)

Gauge Swatch: 4" (10 cm) square

Ch 16.

Row 1: Hdc in third ch from hook **(2 skipped chs count as first hdc)** and in each ch across: 15 hdc.

Rows 2-12: Ch 2 **(counts as first hdc)**, turn; hdc in next hdc and in each hdc across.

Finish off.

STITCH GUIDE

FRONT POST TREBLE CROCHET
(abbreviated FPtr)

YO twice, insert hook from **front** to **back** around post of st indicated *(Fig. 4, page 46)*, YO and pull up a loop (4 loops on hook), (YO and draw through 2 loops on hook) 3 times.

FRONT POST DOUBLE TREBLE CROCHET
(abbreviated FPdtr)

YO 3 times, insert hook from **front** to **back** around post of st indicated *(Fig. 4, page 46)*, YO and pull up a loop (5 loops on hook), (YO and draw through 2 loops on hook) 4 times.

INSTRUCTIONS

BACK

Ch 65.

Row 1 (Right side)**:** Hdc in third ch from hook **(2 skipped chs count as first hdc)** and in each ch across: 64 hdc.

Row 2: Ch 2 **(counts as first hdc, now and throughout)**, turn; hdc in next hdc and in each hdc across.

The diamonds are formed by moving the placement of the FPdtr on each row, and are framed by two columns of FPtr on each side.

Row 3: Ch 2, turn; hdc in next 21 hdc, work FPtr around each hdc one row **below** next 2 hdc, skip next 2 hdc from last hdc made, hdc in next 6 hdc, skip next 2 hdc, work FPdtr around hdc one row **below** next hdc *(Fig. A)*, work FPdtr around next hdc one row **below**, working in **front** of last 2 FPdtr made, work FPdtr around first skipped hdc one row **below** *(Fig. B)*, work FPdtr around second skipped hdc (**Cable made**), skip next 4 hdc from last hdc made, hdc in next 6 hdc, work FPtr around each hdc one row **below** next 2 hdc, skip next 2 hdc from last hdc made, hdc in last 22 hdc: 4 FPtr, 4 FPdtr, and 56 hdc.

Row 4: Ch 2, turn; hdc in next hdc and in each st across: 64 hdc.

Row 5: Ch 2, turn; hdc in next 21 hdc, work FPtr around each of next 2 FPtr one row **below**, skip next 2 hdc from last hdc made, hdc in next 4 hdc, work FPdtr around next FPdtr one row **below** *(Fig. C)*, work FPdtr around next FPdtr, skip next 2 hdc from last hdc made, hdc in next 4 hdc, work FPdtr around next FPdtr one row **below** *(Fig. D)*, work FPdtr around next FPdtr, skip next 2 hdc from last hdc made, hdc in next 4 hdc, work FPtr around each of next 2 FPtr one row **below**, skip next 2 hdc from last hdc made, hdc in last 22 hdc: 4 FPtr, 4 FPdtr, and 56 hdc.

Row 6: Ch 2, turn; hdc in next hdc and in each st across: 64 hdc.

Fig. A

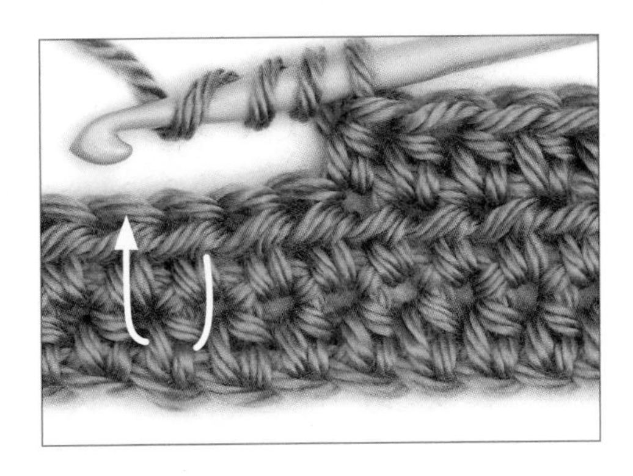

Fig. B

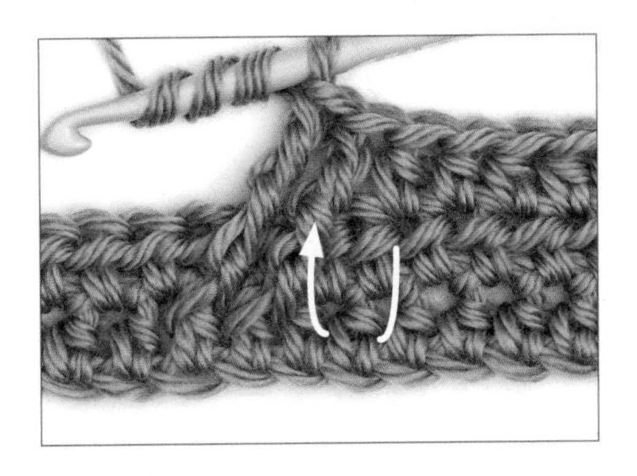

Fig. C

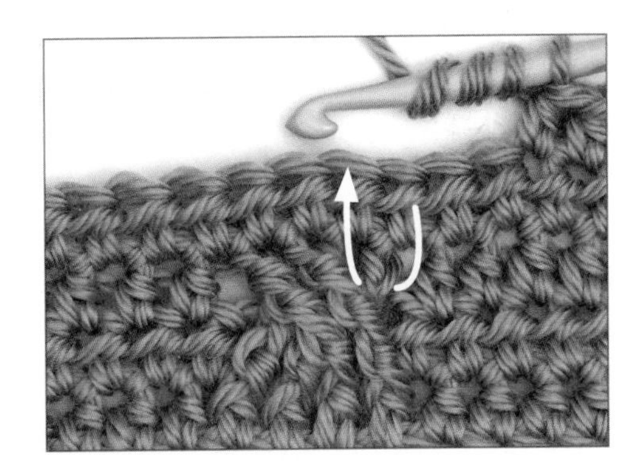

Fig. D

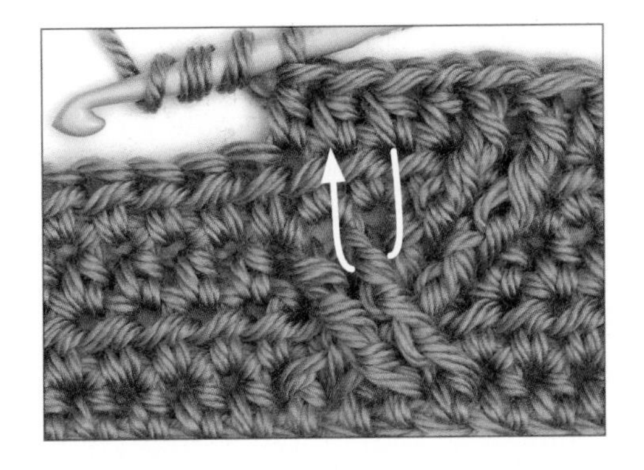

Row 7: Ch 2, turn; hdc in next 21 hdc, work FPtr around each of next 2 FPtr one row **below**, skip next 2 hdc from last hdc made, hdc in next 2 hdc, work FPdtr around each of next 2 FPdtr one row **below**, skip next 2 hdc from last hdc made, hdc in next 8 hdc, work FPdtr around next FPdtr one row **below** ***(Fig. E)***, work FPdtr around next FPdtr, skip next 2 hdc from last hdc made, hdc in next 2 hdc, work FPtr around each of next 2 FPtr one row **below**, skip next 2 hdc from last hdc made, hdc in last 22 hdc: 4 FPtr, 4 FPdtr, and 56 hdc.

Fig. E

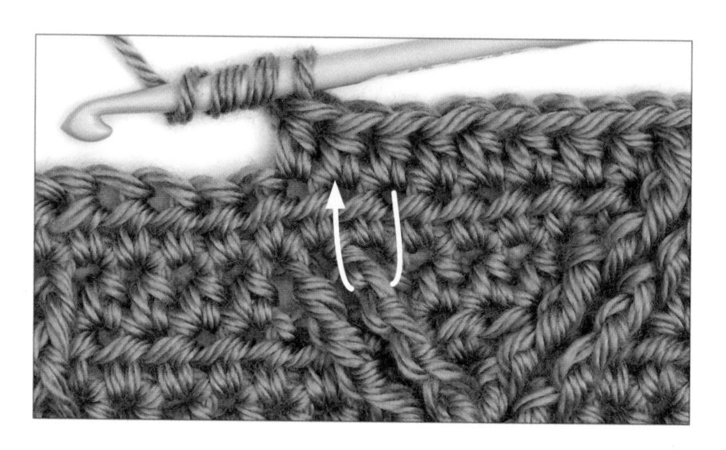

Row 8: Ch 2, turn; hdc in next hdc and in each st across: 64 hdc.

Row 9: Ch 2, turn; hdc in next 21 hdc, work FPtr around each of next 2 FPtr one row **below**, skip next 2 hdc from last hdc made, hdc in next 2 hdc, work FPtr around each of next 2 FPdtr one row **below**, skip next 2 hdc from last hdc made, hdc in next 8 hdc, work FPtr around each of next 2 FPdtr one row **below**, skip next 2 hdc from last hdc made, hdc in next 2 hdc, work FPtr around each of next 2 FPtr one row **below**, skip next 2 hdc from last hdc made, hdc in last 22 hdc: 8 FPtr and 56 hdc.

Row 10: Ch 2, turn; hdc in next hdc and in each st across: 64 hdc.

Row 11: Ch 2, turn; hdc in next 21 hdc, work FPtr around each of next 2 FPtr one row **below**, skip next 2 hdc from last hdc made, hdc in next 4 hdc, work FPdtr around next FPtr one row **below** *(Fig. F)*, work FPdtr around next FPtr, skip next 2 hdc from last hdc made, hdc in next 4 hdc, skip next 2 hdc, work FPdtr around each of next 2 FPtr one row **below**, skip next 2 hdc from last hdc made, hdc in next 4 hdc, work FPtr around each of next 2 FPtr one row **below**, skip next 2 hdc from last hdc made, hdc in last 22 hdc: 4 FPtr, 4 FPdtr, and 56 hdc.

Fig. F

Row 12: Ch 2, turn; hdc in next hdc and in each st across: 64 hdc.

Row 13: Ch 2, turn; hdc in next 21 hdc, work FPtr around each of next 2 FPtr one row **below**, skip next 2 hdc from last hdc made, hdc in next 6 hdc, work FPdtr around each of next 4 FPdtr one row **below**, skip next 4 hdc from last hdc made, hdc in next 6 hdc, work FPtr around each of next 2 FPtr one row **below**, skip next 2 hdc from last hdc made, hdc in last 22 hdc: 4 FPtr, 4 FPdtr, and 56 hdc.

Row 14: Ch 2, turn; hdc in next hdc and in each st across: 64 hdc.

Row 15: Ch 2, turn; hdc in next 21 hdc, work FPtr around each of next 2 FPtr one row **below**, skip next 2 hdc from last hdc made, hdc in next 6 hdc, skip next 2 FPdtr one row **below**, work FPdtr around each of next 2 FPdtr, working in **front** of last 2 FPdtr made, work FPdtr around each of 2 skipped FPdtr (**Cable made**), skip next 4 hdc from last hdc made, hdc in next 6 hdc, work FPtr around each of next 2 FPtr one row **below**, skip next 2 hdc from last hdc made, hdc in last 22 hdc: 4 FPtr, 4 FPdtr, and 56 hdc.

Row 16: Ch 2, turn; hdc in next hdc and in each st across: 64 hdc.

Rows 17-52: Repeat Rows 5-16, 3 times.

Finish off.

FRONT

Work same as Back; do **not** finish off.

ASSEMBLY

Rnd 1: Ch 1, turn; with **wrong** sides of **both** pieces together, Front facing, matching sts on Row 52 and working through **both** thicknesses, (sc evenly across to next corner, 3 sc in corner) 3 times; insert pillow form, sc evenly across to last corner, 3 sc in last corner; join with slip st to first sc.

Rnd 2: Ch 1, do **not** turn; working from **left** to **right**, work reverse sc in each sc around *(Figs. 7a-d, page 47)*; join with slip st to first st, finish off.

Sexton Braid Hat

EASY +

Fits Head Circumference: 20" (51 cm)

SHOPPING LIST

Yarn (Medium Weight) 

[6 ounces, 315 yards (170 grams, 288 meters) per skein]:

- ☐ 1 skein

Crochet Hook

- ☐ Size H (5 mm) **or** size needed for gauge

Additional Supplies

- ☐ Yarn needle

GAUGE INFORMATION

In pattern, 15 sts and 12 rows = 4" (10 cm)

Gauge Swatch: 5¼"w x 3"h (13.25 cm x 7.5 cm)

Work same as Band for 9 rows; do **not** finish off.

STITCH GUIDE

FRONT POST TREBLE CROCHET
(abbreviated FPtr)

YO twice, insert hook from **front** to **back** around post of st indicated *(Fig. 4, page 46)*, YO and pull up a loop (4 loops on hook), (YO and draw through 2 loops on hook) 3 times.

FRONT POST DOUBLE TREBLE CROCHET
(abbreviated FPdtr)

YO 3 times, insert hook from **front** to **back** around post of st indicated *(Fig. 4, page 46)*, YO and pull up a loop (5 loops on hook), (YO and draw through 2 loops on hook) 4 times.

HALF DOUBLE CROCHET 2 TOGETHER
(abbreviated hdc2tog) (uses next 2 hdc)

★ YO, insert hook in **next** hdc, YO and pull up a loop; repeat from ★ once **more**, YO and draw through all 5 loops on hook (**counts as one hdc**).

INSTRUCTIONS

BAND

Ch 22.

Row 1 (Right side)**:** Hdc in back ridge of third ch from hook *(Fig. 1, page 46)* **(2 skipped chs count as first hdc)** and each ch across: 21 hdc.

Row 2: Ch 2 (**counts as first hdc, now and throughout**), turn; hdc in next hdc and in each hdc across.

The next row is made up of cables that use 5 stitches. A hdc is worked between the 2 FPdtr that form the crossed stitches.

Row 3: Ch 2, turn; hdc in next hdc, ★ † skip next 3 hdc, work FPdtr around hdc one row **below** next hdc *(Fig. A)*, work FPdtr around hdc one row **below** next hdc, skip next 2 hdc from last hdc made, hdc in next hdc *(Fig. B)*, working in **front** of last 2 FPdtr made, work FPdtr around first skipped hdc *(Fig. C)*, work FPdtr around second skipped hdc (**Cable made**), skip next 2 hdc from last hdc made †, hdc in next hdc; repeat from ★ once **more**, then repeat from † to † once, hdc in last 2 hdc: 12 FPdtr and 9 hdc.

Row 4: Ch 2, turn; hdc in next hdc and in each st across.

Fig. A

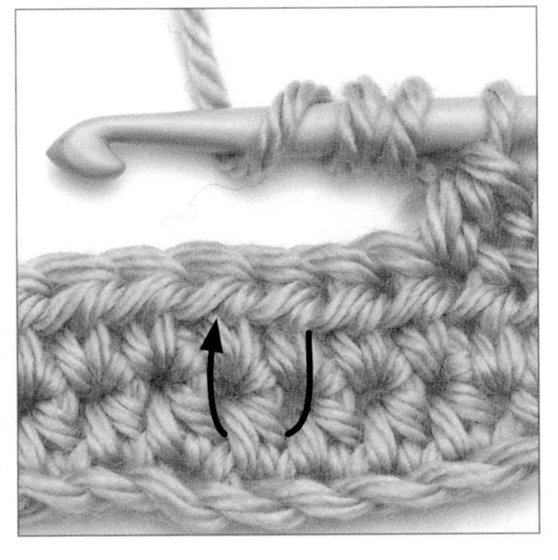

Fig. B

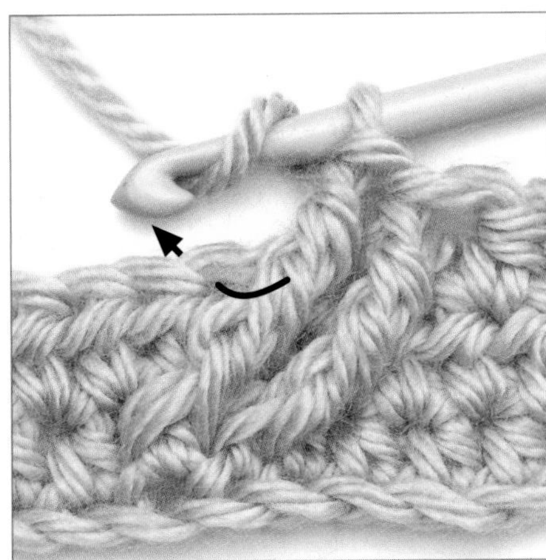

Fig. C

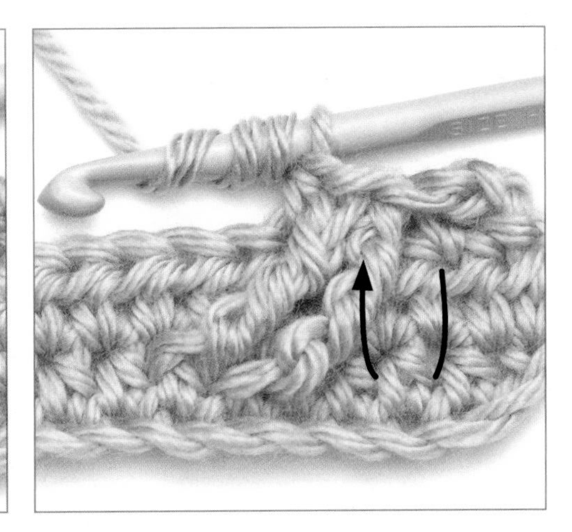

Each of the 2 cables on the next row are centered between 2 of the cables on Row 3; forming a braided look.

Row 5: Ch 2, turn; hdc in next hdc, work FPtr around next FPdtr one row **below** ***(Fig. D)***, work FPtr around next FPdtr, skip next 2 hdc from last hdc made, hdc in next hdc, ★ skip next 2 FPdtr one row **below**, work FPdtr around next FPdtr ***(Fig. E)***, work FPdtr around next FPdtr, skip next 2 hdc from last hdc made, hdc in next hdc, working **behind** last 2 FPdtr made, work FPdtr around first skipped FPdtr one row **below** ***(Fig. F)***, work FPdtr around next skipped FPdtr (**Cable made**), skip next 2 hdc from last hdc made, hdc in next hdc; repeat from ★ once **more**, work FPtr around each of next 2 FPdtr, skip next 2 hdc from last hdc made, hdc in last 2 hdc: 8 FPdtr, 4 FPtr, and 9 hdc.

Row 6: Ch 2, turn; hdc in next hdc and in each st across.

Row 7: Ch 2, turn; hdc in next hdc, ★ † skip next 2 FPsts one row **below**, work FPdtr around each of next 2 FPsts, skip next 2 hdc from last hdc made, hdc in next hdc, working in **front** of last 2 FPdtr made, work FPdtr around each of 2 skipped FPsts (**Cable made**), skip next 2 hdc from last hdc made †, hdc in next hdc; repeat from ★ once **more**, then repeat from † to † once, hdc in last 2 hdc: 12 FPdtr, and 9 hdc.

Fig. D

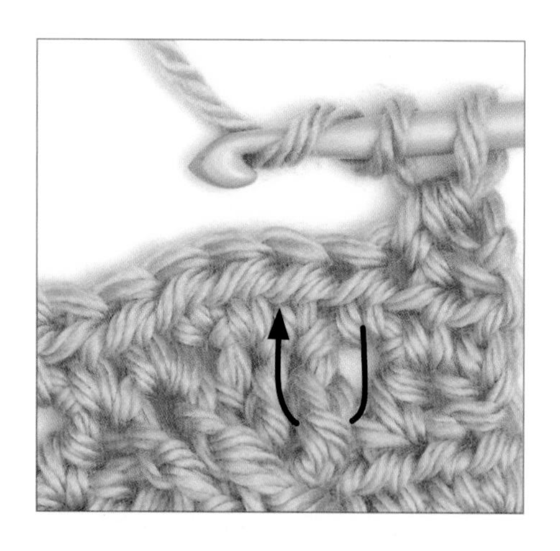

Fig. E

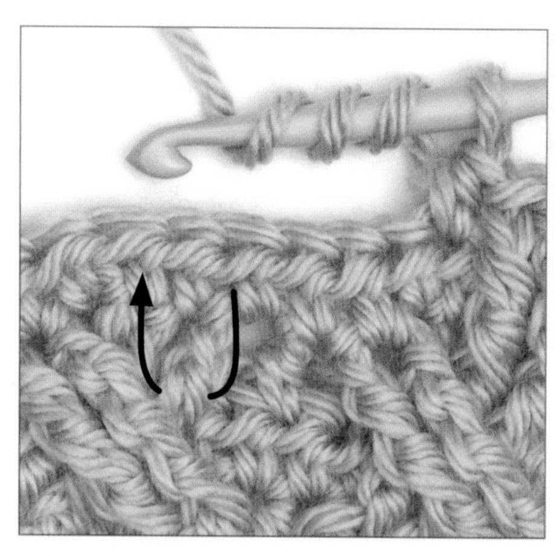

Fig. F

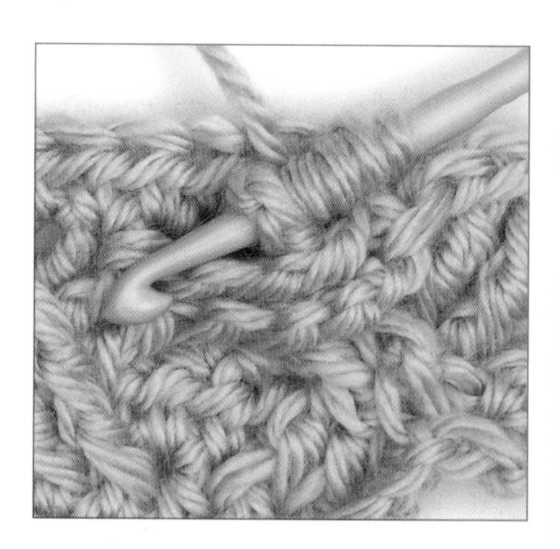

Row 8: Ch 2, turn; hdc in next hdc and in each st across.

Row 9: Ch 2, turn; hdc in next hdc, work FPtr around each of next 2 FPdtr one row **below**, skip next 2 hdc from last hdc made, hdc in next hdc, ★ skip next 2 FPdtr one row **below**, work FPdtr around each of next 2 FPdtr, skip next 2 hdc from last hdc made, hdc in next hdc, working **behind** last 2 FPdtr made, work FPdtr around each of 2 skipped FPdtr **(Cable made)**, skip next 2 hdc from last hdc made, hdc in next hdc; repeat from ★ once **more**, work FPtr around each of next 2 FPdtr, skip next 2 hdc from last hdc made, hdc in last 2 hdc: 8 FPdtr, 4 FPtr, and 9 hdc.

Repeat Rows 6-9 for pattern until Band measures approximately 21" (53.5 cm) from beginning ch, ending by working Row 8.

Finish off, leaving a long end for sewing.

With **wrong** side together, fold Band in half, bringing short edges together. Thread yarn needle with long end and whipstitch short edges together to form a ring *(Fig. 5, page 46)*.

SHAPING

Rnd 1: With **right** side facing, join yarn with hdc at seam *(see Joining With Hdc, page 46)*; work 76 hdc evenly spaced around ends of rows; join with slip st to first hdc: 77 hdc.

Rnd 2: Ch 2, hdc in next 8 hdc, hdc2tog, (hdc in next 9 hdc, hdc2tog) around; join with slip st to first hdc: 70 hdc.

Rnd 3: Ch 2, hdc in next 7 hdc, hdc2tog, (hdc in next 8 hdc, hdc2tog) around; join with slip st to first hdc: 63 hdc.

Rnd 4: Ch 2, hdc in next 6 hdc, hdc2tog, (hdc in next 7 hdc, hdc2tog) around; join with slip st to first hdc: 56 hdc.

Rnd 5: Ch 2, hdc in next hdc, hdc2tog, (hdc in next 2 hdc, hdc2tog) around; join with slip st to first hdc: 42 hdc.

Rnd 6: Ch 2, hdc2tog, (hdc in next hdc, hdc2tog) around; join with slip st to first hdc: 28 hdc.

Rnds 7 and 8: Ch 1, skip first st, hdc in next hdc, hdc2tog around; join with slip st to first hdc: 7 hdc.

Finish off, leaving a long end for sewing.

Thread yarn needle with long end and weave needle through remaining hdc on Rnd 8 ***(Fig. A)***; gather **tightly** to close and secure end.

Fig. A

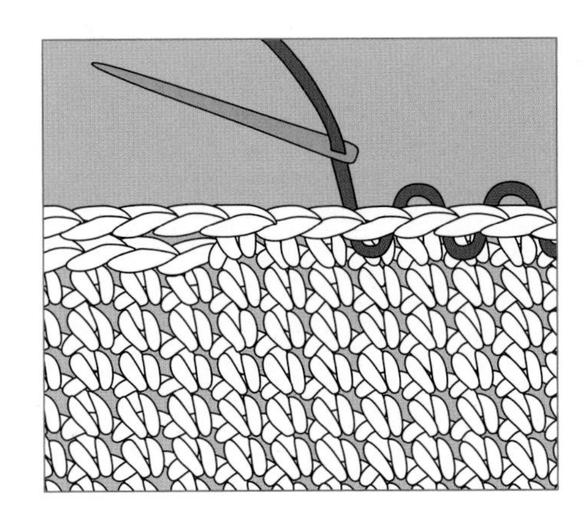

Ballykeeran Fingerless Mitts

EASY +

SHOPPING LIST

Yarn (Medium Weight) MEDIUM 4

[3.5 ounces, 210 yards

(100 grams, 192 meters) per skein**]**:

- ☐ 1 skein

Crochet Hook

- ☐ Size I (5.5 mm)

  or size needed for gauge

SIZE INFORMATION

Finished Hand Circumference:

Small/Medium - 6¼" (16 cm)

Medium/Large - 6¾" (17 cm)

Size Note: We have printed the instructions for the sizes in different colors to make it easier for you to find.

- Size Small/Medium in Blue
- Size Medium/Large in Green

Instruction in Black applies to both sizes.

GAUGE INFORMATION

In pattern, 14 sts and 10 rnds = 4" (10 cm)

Gauge Swatch: 3⅜{3¾}"w (flattened) x 1¾"h/8.5{9.5} cm x 4.5 cm

Work same as Left Mitt through Rnd 4: 24{26} sts.

STITCH GUIDE

FRONT POST DOUBLE CROCHET ***(abbreviated FPdc)***

YO, insert hook from **front** to **back** around post of st indicated *(Fig. 4, page 46)*, YO and pull up a loop (3 loops on hook), (YO and draw through 2 loops on hook) twice.

FRONT POST TREBLE CROCHET ***(abbreviated FPtr)***

YO twice, insert hook from **front** to **back** around post of st indicated *(Fig. 4, page 46)*, YO and pull up a loop (4 loops on hook), (YO and draw through 2 loops on hook) 3 times.

FRONT POST DOUBLE TREBLE CROCHET ***(abbreviated FPdtr)***

YO 3 times, insert hook from **front** to **back** around post of st indicated *(Fig. 4, page 46)*, YO and pull up a loop (5 loops on hook), (YO and draw through 2 loops on hook) 4 times.

INSTRUCTIONS
Left Mitt

Beginning at wrist, ch 24{26} **loosely**; being careful **not** to twist ch, join with slip st to back ridge of first ch to form a ring *(Fig. 4, page 46)*.

Rnd 1 (Right side)**:** Ch 3 **(counts as first dc, now and throughout)**, dc in back ridge of next ch and each ch around; join with slip st to first dc: 24{26} dc.

This cable uses 6 stitches and has a braided look formed by alternating the placement of the crossed stitches.

Rnd 2: Ch 1, sc in same st as joining and in next 5 dc, skip next 2 dc, work FPtr around next dc *(Fig. A)*, work FPtr around next dc, working in **front** of last 2 FPtr made, work FPtr around first skipped dc *(Fig. B)*, work FPtr around second skipped dc (**Cable made**), work FPdc around next dc *(Fig. C)*, work FPdc around next dc, skip next 6 dc from last sc made, sc in last 12{14} dc; join with slip st to first sc: {18-20} sc, 4 FPtr, and 2 FPdc.

Fig. A

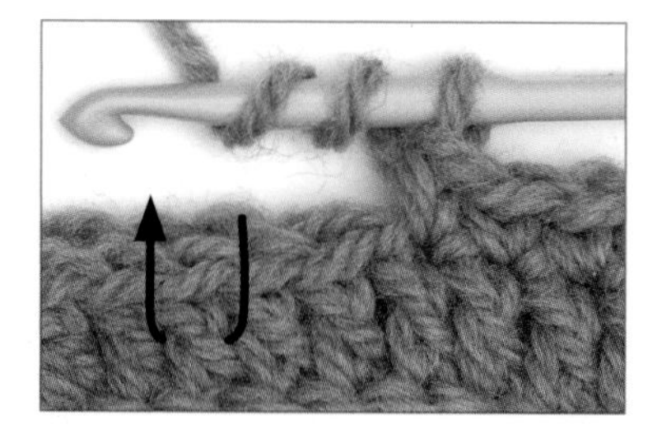

Fig. B

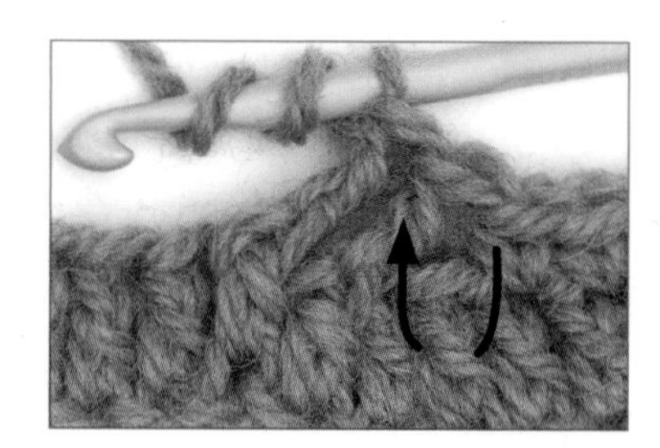

Fig. C

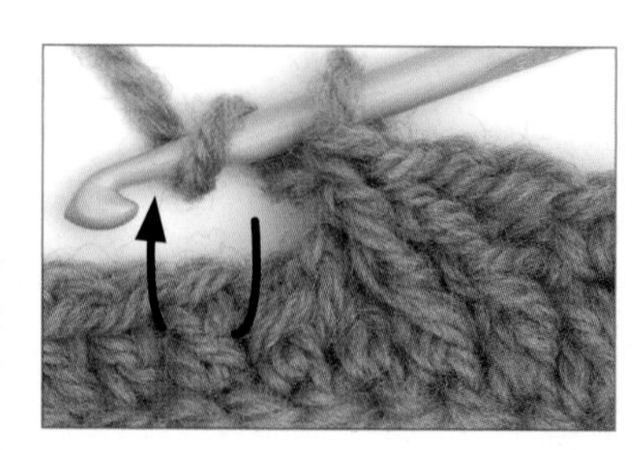

Rnd 3: Ch 3, dc in next st and in each st around; join with slip st to first dc.

Rnd 4: Ch 1, sc in same st as joining and in next 5 dc, work FPtr around next FPtr one rnd **below** ***(Fig. D)***, work FPtr around next FPtr, skip next 2 FPtr, work FPdtr around next FPdc ***(Fig. E)***, work FPdtr around next FPdc, working **behind** last 2 FPdtr made, work FPdtr around first skipped FPtr ***(Fig. F)***, work FPdtr around second skipped FPtr (**Cable made**), skip next 6 dc from last sc made, sc in last 12{14} dc; join with slip st to first sc.

Fig. D

Fig. E

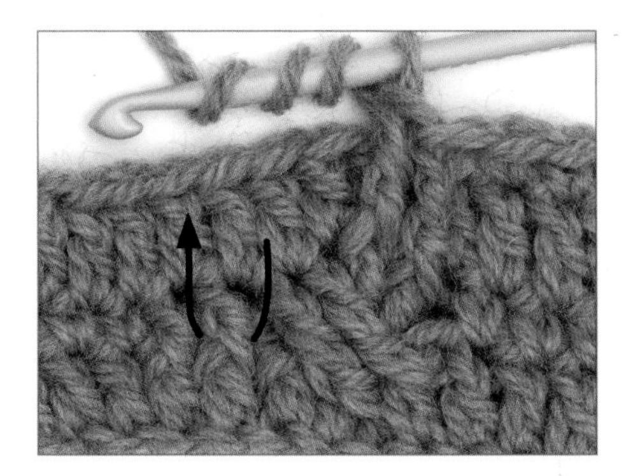

Fig. F

Rnd 5: Ch 3, dc in same st as joining, 2 dc in next sc, dc in next st and in each st around; join with slip st to first dc: 26{28} dc.

Rnd 6: Ch 1, sc in same st as joining and in next 7 dc, skip next 2 FPtr one rnd **below**, work FPdtr around next FPdtr ***(Fig. G)***, work FPdtr around next FPdtr, working in **front** of last 2 FPdtr made, work FPdtr around first skipped FPtr ***(Fig. H)***, work FPdtr around second skipped FPtr (**Cable made**), work FPtr around next FPdtr ***(Fig. I)***, work FPtr around next FPdtr, skip next 6 dc from last sc made, sc in last 12{14} dc; join with slip st to first sc.

Fig. G

Fig. H

Fig. I

Rnd 7: Ch 3, dc in same st as joining and in next 2 sc, 2 dc in next sc, dc in next st and in each st around; join with slip st to first dc: 28{30} dc.

Rnd 8: Ch 1, sc in same st as joining and in next 9 dc, work FPtr around each of next 2 FPdtr one rnd **below**, skip next 2 FPdtr, work FPdtr around each of next 2 FPtr, working **behind** last 2 FPdtr made, work FPdtr around each of 2 skipped FPdtr **(Cable made)**, skip next 6 dc from last sc made, sc in last 12{14} dc; join with slip st to first sc.

Rnd 9: Ch 3, dc in same st as joining and in next 4 sc, 2 dc in next sc, dc in next st and in each st around; join with slip st to first dc: 30{32} dc.

Rnd 10: Ch 1, sc in same st as joining and in next 11 dc, skip next 2 FPtr one rnd **below**, work FPdtr around each of next 2 FPdtr, working in **front** of last 2 FPdtr made, work FPdtr around each of 2 skipped FPtr **(Cable made)**, work FPtr around each of next 2 FPdtr, skip next 6 dc from last sc made, sc in last 12{14} dc; join with slip st to first sc.

Rnd 11: Ch 3, dc in same st as joining and in next 6 sc, 2 dc in next sc, dc in next st and in each st around; join with slip st to first dc: 32{34} dc.

Rnd 12: Ch 1, sc in same st as joining, skip next 10 dc **(thumb opening)**, sc in next 3 dc, work FPtr around each of next 2 FPdtr one rnd **below**, skip next 2 FPdtr, work FPdtr around each of next 2 FPtr, working **behind** last 2 FPdtr made, work FPdtr around each of 2 skipped FPdtr **(Cable made)**, skip next 6 dc from last sc made, sc in last 12{14} dc; join with slip st to first sc: 22{24} sts.

Rnd 13: Ch 3, dc in next st and in each st around; join with slip st to first dc.

Rnd 14: Ch 1, sc in same st as joining and in next 3 dc, skip next 2 FPtr one rnd **below**, work FPdtr around each of next 2 FPdtr, working in **front** of last 2 FPdtr made, work FPdtr around each of 2 skipped FPtr **(Cable made)**, work FPtr around each of next 2 FPdtr, skip next 6 dc from last sc made, sc in last 12{14} dc; join with slip st to first sc, finish off.

Right Mitt

Beginning at wrist, ch 24{26} **loosely**; being careful **not** to twist ch, join with slip st to back ridge of first ch to form a ring.

Rnd 1 (Right side)**:** Ch 3, dc in back ridge of next ch and each ch around; join with slip st to first dc: 24{26} dc.

Rnd 2: Ch 1, sc in same st as joining and in next 11{13} dc, skip next 2 dc, work FPtr around each of next 2 dc, working in **front** of FPtr just made, work FPtr around each of 2 skipped dc **(Cable made)**, work FPdc around each of next 2 dc, skip next 6 dc from last sc made, sc in last 6 dc; join with slip st to first sc.

Rnd 3: Ch 3, dc in next st and in each st around; join with slip st to first dc.

Rnd 4: Ch 1, sc in same st as joining and in next 11{13} dc, work FPtr around each of next 2 FPtr one rnd **below**, skip next 2 FPtr, work FPdtr around each of next 2 FPdc, working **behind** last 2 FPdtr made, work FPdtr around each of 2 skipped FPtr **(Cable made)**, skip next 6 dc from last sc made, sc in last 6 dc; join with slip st to first sc.

Rnd 5: Ch 3, dc in next st and in each st around to last 2 sts, 2 dc in each of last 2 sts; join with slip st to first dc: 26{28} dc.

Rnd 6: Ch 1, sc in same st as joining and in next 11{13} dc, skip next 2 FPtr one rnd **below**, work FPdtr around each of next 2 FPdtr, working in **front** of last 2 FPdtr made, work FPdtr around each of 2 skipped FPtr **(Cable made)**, work FPtr around each of next 2 FPdtr dc, skip next 6 dc from last sc made, sc in last 8 dc; join with slip st to first sc.

Rnd 7: Ch 3, dc in next st and in each st around to last 4 sts, 2 dc in next st, dc in next 2 sts, 2 dc in last st; join with slip st to first dc: 28{30} dc.

Rnd 8: Ch 1, sc in same st as joining and in next 11{13} dc, work FPtr around each of next 2 FPdtr one rnd **below**, skip next 2 FPdtr, work FPdtr around each of next 2 FPtr, working **behind** last 2 FPdtr made, work FPdtr around each of 2 skipped FPdtr **(Cable made)**, skip next 6 dc from last sc made, sc in last 10 dc; join with slip st to first sc.

Rnd 9: Ch 3, dc in next st and in each st around to last 6 sts, 2 dc in next st, dc in next 4 sts, 2 dc in last st; join with slip st to first dc: 30{32} dc.

Rnd 10: Ch 1, sc in same st as joining and in next 11{13} dc, skip next 2 FPtr one rnd **below**, work FPdtr around each of next 2 FPdtr, working in **front** of last 2 FPdtr made, work FPdtr around each of 2 skipped FPtr **(Cable made)**, work FPtr around each of next 2 FPdtr, skip next 6 dc from last sc made, sc in last 12 dc; join with slip st to first sc.

Rnd 11: Ch 3, dc in next st and in each st around to last 8 sts, 2 dc in next st, dc in next 6 sts, 2 dc in last st; join with slip st to first dc: 32{34} dc.

Rnd 12: Ch 1, sc in same st as joining and in next 11{13} dc, work FPtr around each of next 2 FPdtr one rnd **below**, skip next 2 FPdtr, work FPdtr around each of next 2 FPtr, working **behind** last 2 FPdtr made, work FPdtr around each of 2 skipped FPdtr **(Cable made)**, skip next 6 dc from last sc made, sc in next 3 dc, skip next 10 dc **(thumb opening)**, sc in last dc; join with slip st to first sc: 22{24} sts.

Rnd 13: Ch 3, dc in next st and in each st around; join with slip st to first dc.

Rnd 14: Ch 1, sc in same st as joining and in next 11{13} dc, skip next 2 FPtr one rnd **below**, work FPdtr around each of next 2 FPdtr one rnd **below**, working in **front** of last 2 FPdtr made, work FPdtr around each of 2 skipped FPtr **(Cable made)**, work FPtr around each of next 2 FPdtr, skip next 6 dc from last sc made, sc in last 4 dc; join with slip st to first sc, finish off.

Heirloom Aran Afghan

INTERMEDIATE

Finished Size: 51" x 62½" (129.5 cm x 159 cm)

SHOPPING LIST

Yarn (Medium Weight) 

[3.5 ounces, 170 yards (100 grams, 156 meters) per skein**]**:

- ☐ 27 skeins

Crochet Hook

- ☐ Size I (5.5 mm) **or** size needed for gauge

GAUGE INFORMATION

In pattern, 14 sts and 12 rows = 4" (10 cm)

Gauge Swatch: 4" (10 cm) square

Ch 15.

Row 1: Hdc in third ch from hook **(2 skipped ch count as first hdc)** and in each ch across: 14 hdc.

Rows 2-12: Ch 2 **(counts as first hdc)**, turn; hdc in next hdc and in each hdc across.

Finish off.

STITCH GUIDE

BACK POST TREBLE CROCHET

(abbreviated BPtr)

YO twice, insert hook from **back** to **front** around post of st indicated *(Fig. 4, page 46)*, YO and pull up a loop (4 loops on hook), (YO and draw through 2 loops on hook) 3 times.

FRONT POST TREBLE CROCHET

(abbreviated FPtr)

YO twice, insert hook from **front** to **back** around post of st indicated *(Fig. 4, page 46)*, YO and pull up a loop (4 loops on hook), (YO and draw through 2 loops on hook) 3 times.

FRONT POST DOUBLE TREBLE CROCHET

(abbreviated FPdtr)

YO 3 times, insert hook from **front** to **back** around post of st indicated *(Fig. 4, page 46)*, YO and pull up a loop (5 loops on hook), (YO and draw through 2 loops on hook) 4 times.

POPCORN (uses one hdc)

5 Dc in hdc indicated, drop loop from hook, insert hook in first dc of 5-dc group, hook dropped loop and pull though st.

INSTRUCTIONS

BODY

Ch 176; place marker in second ch from hook for Edging placement.

Row 1 (Right side): Hdc in third ch from hook **(2 skipped chs count as first hdc)** and in each ch across: 175 hdc.

Row 2: Ch 2 **(counts as first hdc, now and throughout)**, turn; hdc in next hdc and in each hdc across.

Row 3: Ch 2, turn; hdc in next hdc, ★ † (work FPtr around each hdc one row **below** next 3 hdc, work BPtr around each hdc one row **below** next 3 hdc) 4 times, hdc in next 2 hdc on Row 2 †, work FPtr around each hdc one row **below** next 2 hdc, skip next 2 hdc from last hdc made, hdc in next 6 hdc, skip next 3 hdc, work FPdtr around each hdc one row **below** next 2 hdc, skip next 2 hdc from last hdc made, hdc in next hdc, working in **front** of last FPdtr made, work FPdtr around each hdc one row **below** first 2 skipped hdc **(Cable made)**, skip next 2 hdc from last hdc made, hdc in next 6 hdc, work FPtr around each hdc one row **below** next 2 hdc, skip next 2 hdc from last hdc made, hdc in next 2 hdc; repeat from ★ 2 times **more**, then repeat from † to † once: 60 FPtr, 48 BPtr, 12 FPdtr, and 55 hdc.

Row 4: Ch 2, turn; hdc in next hdc and in each st across: 175 hdc.

Row 5: Ch 2, turn; hdc in next hdc, ★ † (work BPtr around each of next 3 FPtr one row **below**, work FPtr around each of next 3 BPtr one row **below**) 4 times, hdc in next 2 hdc on previous row †, work FPtr around each of next 2 FPtr one row **below**, skip next 2 hdc from last hdc made, hdc in next 4 hdc, work FPdtr around each of next 2 FPdtr one row **below**, skip next 2 hdc from last hdc made, hdc in next 5 hdc, work FPdtr around each of next 2 FPdtr one row **below**, skip next 2 hdc from last hdc made, hdc in next 4 hdc, work FPtr around each of next 2 FPtr one row **below**, skip next 2 hdc from last hdc made, hdc in next 2 hdc; repeat from ★ 2 times **more**, then repeat from † to † once: 60 FPtr, 48 BPtr, 12 FPdtr, and 55 hdc.

Row 6: Ch 2, turn; hdc in next hdc and in each st across: 175 hdc.

Row 7: Ch 2, turn; hdc in next hdc, ★ † (work FPtr around each of next 3 BPtr one row **below**, work BPtr around each of next 3 FPtr one row **below**) 4 times, hdc in next 2 hdc on previous row †, work FPtr around each of next 2 FPtr one row **below**, skip next 2 hdc from last hdc made, hdc in next 2 hdc, work FPdtr around each of next 2 FPdtr one row **below**, skip next 2 hdc from last hdc made, hdc in next 9 hdc, work FPdtr around each of next 2 FPdtr one row **below**, skip next 2 hdc from last hdc made, hdc in next 2 hdc, work FPtr around each of next 2 FPtr one row **below**, skip next 2 hdc from last hdc made, hdc in next 2 hdc; repeat from ★ 2 times **more**, then repeat from † to † once: 60 FPtr, 48 BPtr, 12 FPdtr, and 55 hdc.

Row 8: Ch 2, turn; hdc in next hdc and in each st across: 175 hdc.

Row 9: Ch 2, turn; hdc in next hdc, ★ † (work BPtr around each of next 3 FPtr one row **below**, work FPtr around each of next 3 BPtr one row **below**) 4 times, hdc in next 2 hdc on previous row †, work FPtr around each of next 2 FPtr one row **below**, skip next 2 hdc from last hdc made, hdc in next 2 hdc, work FPtr around each of next 2 FPdtr one row **below,** skip next 2 hdc from last hdc made, hdc in next 4 hdc, work Popcorn in next hdc, hdc in next 4 hdc, work FPtr around each of next 2 FPdtr one row **below**, skip next 2 hdc from last hdc made, hdc in next 2 hdc, work FPtr around each of next 2 FPtr one row **below**, skip next 2 hdc from last hdc made, hdc in next 2 hdc; repeat from ★ 2 times **more**, then repeat from † to † once: 72 FPtr, 48 BPtr, 3 Popcorns, and 52 hdc.

Row 10: Ch 2, turn; hdc in next hdc and in each st across: 175 hdc.

Row 11: Ch 2, turn; hdc in next hdc, ★ † (work FPtr around each of next 3 BPtr one row **below**, work BPtr around each each of next 3 FPtr one row **below**) 4 times, hdc in next 2 hdc on previous row †, work FPtr around each of next 2 FPtr one row **below**, skip next 2 hdc from last hdc made, hdc in next 4 hdc, work FPdtr around each of next 2 FPtr one row **below**, skip next 2 hdc from last hdc made, hdc in next 5 hdc, work FPdtr around each of next 2 FPtr one row **below**, skip next 2 hdc from last hdc made, hdc in next 4 hdc, work FPtr around each of next 2 FPtr one row **below**, skip next 2 hdc from last hdc made, hdc in next 2 hdc; repeat from ★ 2 times **more**, then repeat from † to † once: 60 FPtr, 48 BPtr, 12 FPdtr, and 55 hdc.

Row 12: Ch 2, turn; hdc in next hdc and in each st across: 175 hdc.

Row 13: Ch 2, turn; hdc in next hdc, ★ † (work BPtr around each of next 3 FPtr one row **below**, work FPtr around each of next 3 BPtr one row **below**) 4 times, hdc in next 2 hdc on previous row †, work FPtr around each of next 2 FPtr one row **below**, skip next 2 hdc from last hdc made, hdc in next 6 hdc, work FPdtr around each of next 2 FPdtr one row **below**, skip next 2 hdc from last hdc made, hdc in next hdc, work FPdtr around each of next 2 FPdtr one row **below**, skip next 2 hdc from last hdc made, hdc in next 6 hdc, work FPtr around each of next 2 FPtr one row **below**, skip next 2 hdc from last hdc made, hdc in next 2 hdc; repeat from ★ 2 times **more**, then repeat from † to † once: 60 FPtr, 48 BPtr, 12 FPdtr, and 55 hdc.

Row 14: Ch 2, turn; hdc in next hdc and in each st across: 175 hdc.

Row 15: Ch 2, turn; hdc in next hdc, ★ † (work FPtr around each of next 3 BPtr one row **below**, work BPtr around each of next 3 FPtr one row **below**) 4 times, hdc in next 2 hdc on previous row †, work FPtr around each of next 2 FPtr one row **below**, skip next 2 hdc from last hdc made, hdc in next 6 hdc, skip next 2 FPdtr one row **below**, work FPdtr around each of next 2 FPdtr, skip next 2 hdc from last hdc made, hdc in next hdc, working in **front** of last FPdtr made, work FPdtr around each of 2 skipped FPdtr, skip next 2 hdc from last hdc made, hdc in next 6 hdc, work FPtr around each of next 2 FPtr one row **below**, skip next 2 hdc from last hdc made, hdc in next 2 hdc; repeat from ★ 2 times **more**, then repeat from † to † once: 60 FPtr, 48 BPtr, 12 FPdtr, and 55 hdc.

Repeat Rows 4-15 until Body measures approximately 61½" (156 cm) from beginning ch, ending by working Row 4; do **not** finish off.

EDGING

Rnd 1: Ch 1, turn; sc evenly around working 3 sc in each corner; join with slip st to first sc.

Rnd 2: Ch 1, do **not** turn; working from **left** to **right**, work reverse sc in each sc around *(Figs. 7a-d, page 47)*; join with slip st to first st, finish off.

Innisberry Pullover

INTERMEDIATE

SHOPPING LIST

Yarn (Medium Weight) 

[3.5 ounces, 210 yards
(100 grams, 192 meters) per skein]:

☐ {8-9}{10-11-12} skeins

Crochet Hooks

☐ Size H (5 mm) **and**

☐ Size I (5.5 mm)

or sizes needed for gauge

Additional Supplies

☐ Yarn needle

SIZE INFORMATION

Size:	Finished Chest Measurement:
Small	36½" (92.5 cm)
Medium	40" (101.5 cm)
Large	44" (112 cm)
X-Large	47½" (120.5 cm)
2X-Large	52½" (133.5 cm)

Size Note: We have printed the instructions for the sizes in different colors to make it easier for you to find:

- Size Small in Blue
- Size Medium in Pink
- Size Large in Green
- Size X-Large in Red
- Size 2X-Large in Purple

Instructions in Black apply to all sizes.

GAUGE INFORMATION

With larger size hook,

13 hdc and 11 rows = 4" (10 cm)

Cable Panel (29 sts) = 9" (22.75 cm) wide

Gauge Swatch: 4" (10 cm) square

With larger size hook, ch 14.

Row 1: Hdc in third ch from hook **(2 skipped chs count as first hdc)** and in each ch across: 13 hdc.

Rows 2-10: Ch 2 **(counts as first hdc)**, turn; hdc in next hdc and in each hdc across.

Finish off.

STITCH GUIDE

FRONT POST TREBLE CROCHET *(abbreviated FPtr)*

YO twice, insert hook from **front** to **back** around post of st indicated *(Fig. 4, page 46)*, YO and pull up a loop (4 loops on hook), (YO and draw through 2 loops on hook) 3 times.

FRONT POST DOUBLE TREBLE CROCHET *(abbreviated FPdtr)*

YO 3 times, insert hook from **front** to **back** around post of st indicated *(Fig. 4, page 46)*, YO and pull up a loop (5 loops on hook), (YO and draw through 2 loops on hook) 4 times.

POPCORN (uses one hdc)

5 Dc in hdc indicated, drop loop from hook, insert hook in first dc of 5-dc group, hook dropped loop and pull though st.

HALF DOUBLE CROCHET 2 TOGETHER *(abbreviated hdc2tog)* (uses next 2 sts)

★ YO, insert hook in **next** st, YO and pull up a loop; repeat from ★ once **more**, YO and draw through all 5 loops on hook **(counts as one hdc)**.

CABLE PANEL (uses 29 sts)

Row 1: Work FPtr around each st one row **below** next 2 hdc, skip next 2 hdc from last hdc made, hdc in next 3 hdc, work FPtr around each st one row **below** next 2 hdc, skip next 2 hdc from last hdc made, hdc in next 2 hdc, † skip next 3 hdc, work FPdtr around each st one row **below** next 2 hdc, skip next 2 hdc from last hdc made, hdc in next hdc, working in **front** of last 2 FPdtr made, work FPdtr around each st one row **below** first 2 skipped hdc, skip next 2 hdc from last hdc made †, hdc in next hdc, repeat from † to † once, hdc in next 2 hdc, work FPtr around each st one row **below** next 2 hdc, skip next 2 hdc from last hdc made, hdc in next 3 hdc, work FPtr around each st one row **below** next 2 hdc, skip next 2 hdc from last hdc made.

Row 2: Hdc in each st across.

Row 3: Work FPtr around each of next 2 FPtr one row **below**, skip next 2 hdc from last hdc made, hdc in next hdc, work Popcorn in next hdc, hdc in next hdc, work FPtr around each of next 2 FPtr one row **below**, skip next 2 hdc from last hdc made, hdc in next 2 hdc, work FPtr around each of next 2 FPdtr one row **below**, skip next 2 hdc from last hdc made, hdc in next hdc, skip next 2 FPdtr one row **below**, work FPdtr around each of next 2 FPdtr, skip next 2 hdc from last hdc made, hdc in next hdc, working **behind** last 2 FPdtr made, work FPdtr around each of skipped 2 FPdtr one row **below**, skip next 2 hdc from last hdc made, hdc in next hdc, work FPtr around each of next 2 FPdtr one row **below (Cable made)**, skip next 2 hdc from last hdc made, hdc in next 2 hdc, work FPtr around each of next 2 FPtr one row **below**, skip next 2 hdc from last hdc made, hdc in next hdc, work Popcorn in next hdc, hdc in next hdc, work FPtr around each of next 2 FPtr one row **below**, skip next 2 hdc from last hdc made.

Row 4: Hdc in each st across.

Repeat Rows 1-4 for pattern.

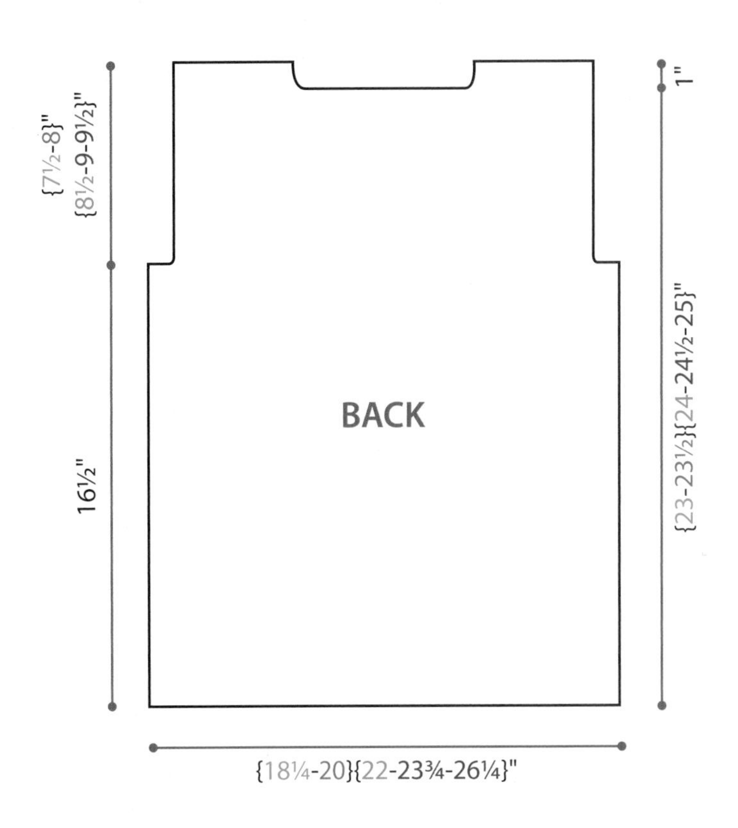

INSTRUCTIONS

BACK

With larger size hook, ch {60-66}{72-78-86}.

Row 1 (Right side)**:** Hdc in back ridge of third ch from hook *(Fig. 1, page 46)* **(2 skipped chs count as first hdc, now and throughout)** and in each ch across: {59-65}{71-77-85} hdc.

Row 2: Ch 2 **(counts as first hdc, now and throughout)**, turn; hdc in next hdc and in each hdc across.

Begin working the Cable Panel across the center 29 stitches.

All wrong side rows of both the Cable Panel and the side stitches are the same.

Row 3: Ch 2, turn; hdc in next {14-17}{20-23-27} hdc, work Row 1 of Cable Panel, hdc in last {15-18}{21-24-28} hdc: 8 FPtr, 8 FPdtr, and {43-49}{55-61-69} hdc.

Row 4: Ch 2, turn; hdc in next st and in each st across: {59-65}{71-77-85} hdc.

Row 5: Ch 2, turn; hdc in next {14-17}{20-23-27} hdc, work Row 3 of Cable Panel, hdc in last {15-18}{21-24-28} hdc: 12 FPtr, 4 FPdtr, 2 Popcorns, and {41-47}{53-59-67} hdc.

Row 6: Ch 2, turn; hdc in next st and in each st across: {59-65}{71-77-85} hdc.

Repeat Rows 3-6 for pattern until Back measures approximately 16" (40.5 cm) from beginning ch, ending by working a **wrong** side row; do **not** finish off.

ARMHOLE SHAPING

Maintain established pattern throughout.

Row 1: Turn; slip st in first {3-4}{4-4-6} hdc, ch 2, work across to last {2-3}{3-3-5} hdc, leave remaining hdc unworked: {55-59}{65-71-75} sts.

Row 2: Turn; slip st in first {3-3}{3-4-4} hdc, ch 2, hdc in next st and in each st across to last {2-2}{2-3-3} hdc, leave remaining hdc unworked: {51-55}{61-65-69} hdc.

Rows 3 thru {4-5}{6-6-6}: Ch 2, turn; hdc2tog, work across to last 3 hdc, hdc2tog, hdc in last hdc: {47-49}{53-57-61} sts.

Work even until Armholes measure approximately {6½-7}{7½-8-8½}"/{16.5-18}{19-20.5-21.5} cm, ending by working a **wrong** side row; do **not** finish off.

Right Neck Shaping

Row 1: Ch 2, turn; work across next {11-12}{14-16-18} sts, leave remaining sts unworked: {12-13}{15-17-19} sts.

Row 2: Ch 2, turn; hdc2tog, hdc in next st and in each st across: {11-12}{14-16-18} hdc.

Work even until piece measures approximately {24-24½}{25-25½-26}"/{61-62}{63.5-65-66} cm from beginning ch, ending by working a **wrong** side row; finish off leaving a long end for sewing.

Left Neck Shaping

Row 1: With **right** side facing, skip next 23 hdc from Right Neck Shaping and join yarn with hdc in next st *(see Joining With Hdc, page 46)*; work across: {12-13}{15-17-19} sts.

Row 2: Ch 2, turn; hdc in next hdc and in each st across to last 3 hdc, hdc2tog, hdc in last hdc: {11-12}{14-16-18} hdc.

Work even until piece measures same as Left Neck Shaping; finish off leaving a long end for sewing.

FRONT

Work same as Back until Armholes measure approximately {4½-5}{5½-6-6½}"/{11.5-12.5}{14-15-16.5} cm, ending by working a **wrong** side row; do **not** finish off: {47-49}{53-57-61} hdc.

Left Neck Shaping

Row 1: Ch 2, turn; work across next {15-16}{18-20-22} sts, leave remaining sts unworked: {16-17}{19-21-23} sts.

Row 2: Turn; slip st in first 3 sts, ch 2, hdc in next st and in each st across: {14-15}{17-19-21} hdc.

Row 3: Ch 2, turn; work across to last 3 sts, hdc2tog, hdc in last st: {13-14}{16-18-20} sts.

Row 4: Ch 2, turn; hdc2tog, hdc in next st and in each st across: {12-13}{15-17-19} hdc.

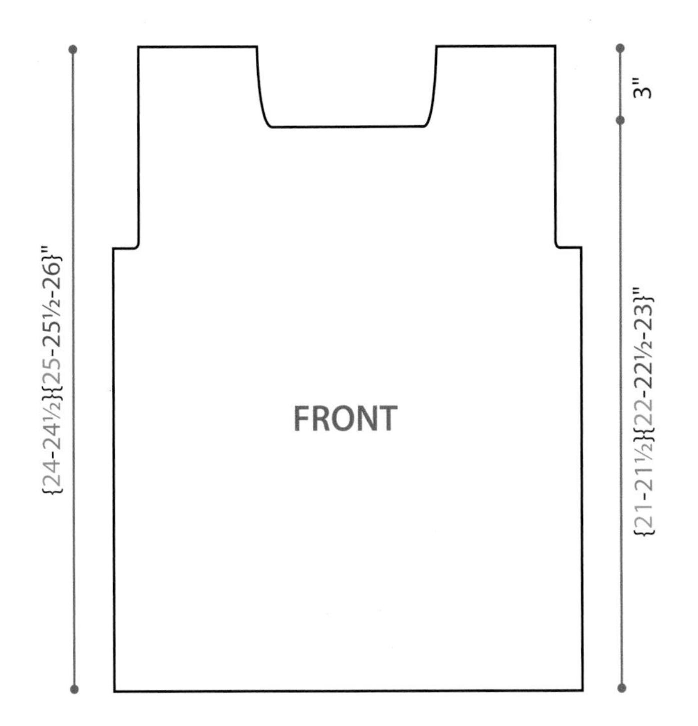

Row 5: Ch 2, turn; work across to last 3 sts, hdc2tog, hdc in last st: {11-12}{14-16-18} sts.

Work even until piece measures same as Back, ending by working a **wrong** side row; finish off.

Right Neck Shaping

Row 1: With **right** side facing, skip next 15 hdc from Left Neck Shaping and join yarn with hdc in next st; work across: {16-17}{19-21-23} sts.

Row 2: Ch 2, turn; hdc in next hdc and in each st across to last 2 sts, leave remaining 2 sts unworked: {14-15}{17-19-21} hdc.

Row 3: Ch 2, turn; hdc2tog, work across: {13-14}{16-18-20} sts.

Row 4: Ch 2, turn; hdc in next st and in each st across to last 3 sts, hdc2tog, hdc in last st: {12-13}{15-17-19} hdc.

Row 5: Ch 2, turn; hdc2tog, work across: {11-12}{14-16-18} sts.

Work even until piece measures same as Left Neck Shaping, ending by working a **wrong** side row; finish off.

SLEEVE

BODY

With larger size hook, ch 34.

Row 1 (Right side)**:** Hdc in third ch from hook **(2 skipped chs count as first hdc)** and in each ch across: 33 hdc.

Row 2: Ch 2, turn; hdc in next hdc and in each hdc across.

Row 3: Ch 2, turn; hdc in next hdc, work Row 1 of Cable Panel, skip next 2 hdc from last hdc made, hdc in last 2 hdc.

Row 4: Ch 2, turn; hdc in next st and in each st across.

Row 5 (Increase row)**:** Ch 2, turn; 2 hdc in next hdc, work Row 3 of Cable Panel, 2 hdc in next hdc, hdc in last hdc: 35 hdc.

Row 6: Ch 2, turn; hdc in next st and in each st across.

Maintaining established pattern throughout.

Increase one stitch at each edge in same manner, every other row, {0-0}{0-0-2} times ***(see Zeros, page 46)***; every fourth row, {0-0}{3-9-8} times; every sixth row, {0-6}{4-0-0} times; every eighth row, {2-0}{0-0-0} times; every tenth row, {2-0}{0-0-0} times: {43-47}{49-53-55} hdc.

Work even until Body measures approximately 18½" (47 cm) from beginning ch, ending by working a **wrong** side row; do **not** finish off.

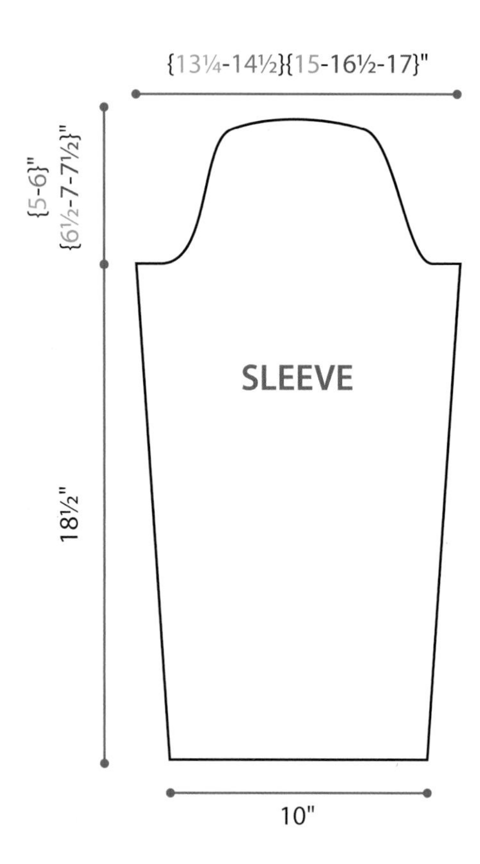

CAP SHAPING

Row 1: Turn; slip st in first {3-4}{4-4-6} hdc, ch 2, work across to last {2-3}{3-3-5} hdc, leave remaining hdc unworked: {39-41}{43-47-45} sts.

Rows 2 thru {5-6}{7-7-10}: Ch 2, turn; hdc2tog, work across to last 3 sts, hdc2tog, hdc in last st: {31-31}{31-35-27} sts.

Work even until Cap Shaping measures approximately {3¼-4¼}{4¾-5-6}"/{8.5-11}{12-12.5-15} cm, ending by working a **wrong** side row.

Next {3-3}{3-4-2} Rows: Ch 2, turn; hdc2tog twice, work across to last 5 sts, hdc2tog twice, hdc in last st: 19 sts.

Last 2 Rows: Turn; slip st in first 4 sts, ch 2, work across to last 3 sts, leave remaining 3 sts unworked: 7 sts.

Finish off.

FINISHING

Whipstitch shoulder seams *(Fig. 7, page 46)*.

NECK RIBBING

Foundation Rnd: With **right** side facing and using smaller size hook, join yarn with sc at center of Back neck *(see Joining With Sc, page 46)*; sc evenly around neck edge working an even number of sc; join with slip st to first sc.

Row 1: Ch 12, sc in back ridge of second ch from hook and each ch across, slip st in first 2 sc on Foundation Rnd: 13 sts.

Row 2: Turn; skip first 2 slip sts, sc in Back Loop Only of each sc across *(Fig. 5, page 46)*: 11 sc.

Rnd 3: Turn; sc in Back loop Only of each sc across, slip st in **both** loops of next 2 sc on Foundation Rnd: 13 sts.

Repeat Rows 2 and 3 around, ending by working Row 2; finish off leaving a long end for sewing.

Whipstitch Neck Ribbing seam.

Sew Sleeves to pullover, placing center of last row on Sleeve Cap at shoulder seam and matching slip sts of Sleeve to unworked slip sts on Armhole.

Weave side and underarm in one continuous seam *(Fig. 8, page 47)*.

General Instructions

ABBREVIATIONS

BPtr	Back Post treble crochet(s)
ch(s)	chain(s)
cm	centimeters
dc	double crochet(s)
FPdc	Front Post double crochet(s)
FPdtr	Front Post double treble crochet(s)
FPst(s)	Front Post stitch(es)
FPtr	Front Post treble crochet(s)
hdc	half double crochet(s)
hdc2tog	half double crochet 2 together
mm	millimeters
Rnd(s)	Round(s)
sc	single crochet(s)
st(s)	stitch(es)
YO	yarn over

CROCHET TERMINOLOGY		
UNITED STATES		INTERNATIONAL
slip stitch (slip st)	=	single crochet (sc)
single crochet (sc)	=	double crochet (dc)
half double crochet (hdc)	=	half treble crochet (htr)
double crochet (dc)	=	treble crochet(tr)
treble crochet (tr)	=	double treble crochet (dtr)
double treble crochet (dtr)	=	triple treble crochet (ttr)
triple treble crochet (tr tr)	=	quadruple treble crochet (qtr)
skip	=	miss

SYMBOLS & TERMS

★ — work instructions following ★ as many **more** times as indicated in addition to the first time.

† to † — work all instructions from first † to second † **as many** times as specified.

( ) or [ ] — work enclosed instructions **as many** times as specified by the number immediately following **or** work all enclosed instructions in the stitch or space indicated **or** contains explanatory remarks.

colon (:) — the number(s) given after a colon at the end of a row or round denote(s) the number of stitches you should have on that row or round.

work even — work without increasing or decreasing in the established pattern.

GAUGE

Exact gauge is essential for proper size. Before beginning your project, make the sample swatch given in the individual instructions in the yarn and hook specified. After completing the swatch, measure it, counting your stitches and rows or rounds carefully. If your swatch is larger or smaller than specified, **make another, changing hook size to get the correct gauge.** Keep trying until you find the size hook that will give you the specified gauge.

Yarn Weight Symbol & Names	LACE 0	SUPER FINE 1	FINE 2	LIGHT 3	MEDIUM 4	BULKY 5	SUPER BULKY 6
Type of Yarns in Category	Fingering, 10-count crochet thread	Sock, Fingering Baby	Sport, Baby	DK, Light Worsted	Worsted, Afghan, Aran	Chunky, Craft, Rug	Bulky, Roving
Crochet Gauge* Ranges in Single Crochet to 4" (10 cm)	32-42 double crochets**	21-32 sts	16-20 sts	12-17 sts	11-14 sts	8-11 sts	5-9 sts
Advised Hook Size Range	Steel*** 6,7,8 Regular hook B-1	B-1 to E-4	E-4 to 7	7 to I-9	I-9 to K-10.5	K-10.5 to M-13	M-13 and larger

*GUIDELINES ONLY: The chart above reflects the most commonly used gauges and hook sizes for specific yarn categories.

** Lace weight yarns are usually crocheted on larger-size hooks to create lacy openwork patterns. Accordingly, a gauge range is difficult to determine. Always follow the gauge stated in your pattern.

*** Steel crochet hooks are sized differently from regular hooks–the higher the number the smaller the hook, which is the reverse of regular hook sizing.

ZEROS

To consolidate the length of an involved pattern, zeros are sometimes used so that all sizes can be combined. For example, increase every other row, {0-0}{0-0-2} times means the first, second, third, and fourth size would do nothing while the largest size would increase 2 times.

JOINING WITH SC

When instructed to join with sc, begin with a slip knot on the hook. Insert the hook in the stitch or space indicated, YO and pull up a loop, YO and draw through both loops on the hook.

JOINING WITH HDC

When instructed to join with hdc, begin with a slip knot on the hook. YO, holding loop on the hook, insert the hook in the stitch or space indicated, YO and pull up a loop, YO and draw through all 3 loops on hook.

BACK RIDGE

Work only in loops indicated by arrows *(Fig. 1)*.

Fig. 1

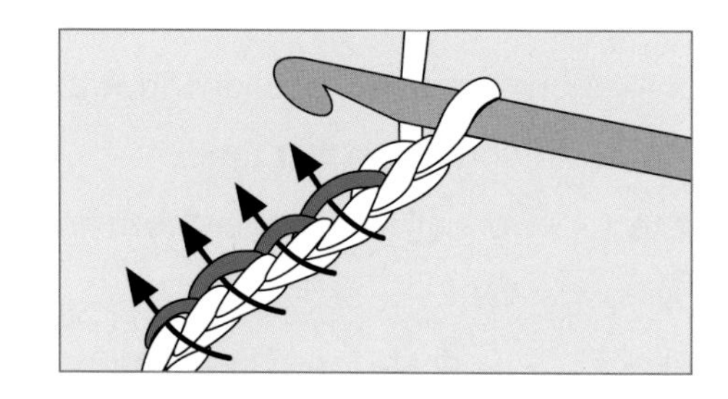

BACK LOOP ONLY

Work only in loop(s) indicated by arrow *(Fig. 2)*.

Fig. 2

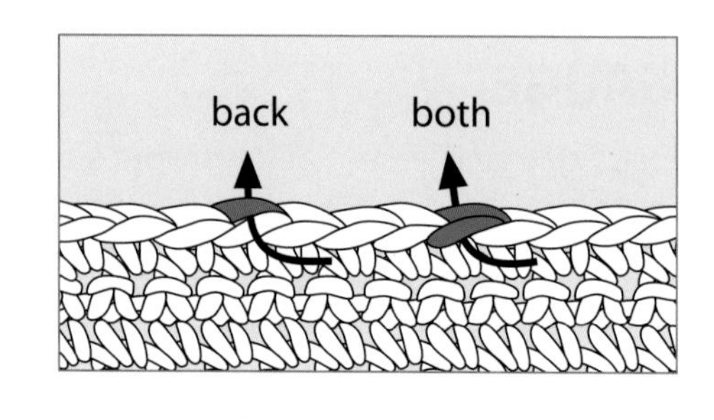

FREE LOOPS OF A CHAIN

When instructed to work in free loops of a chain, work in loop indicated by arrow *(Fig. 3)*.

Fig. 3

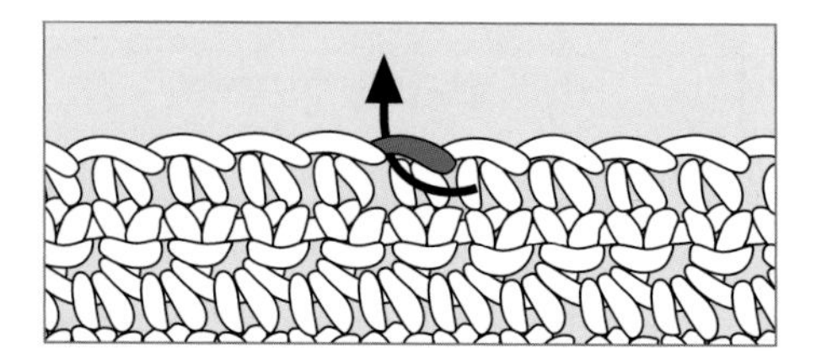

POST STITCHES

work around the post of the stitch indicated, inserting the hook in the direction of the arrow *(Fig. 4)*.

Fig. 4

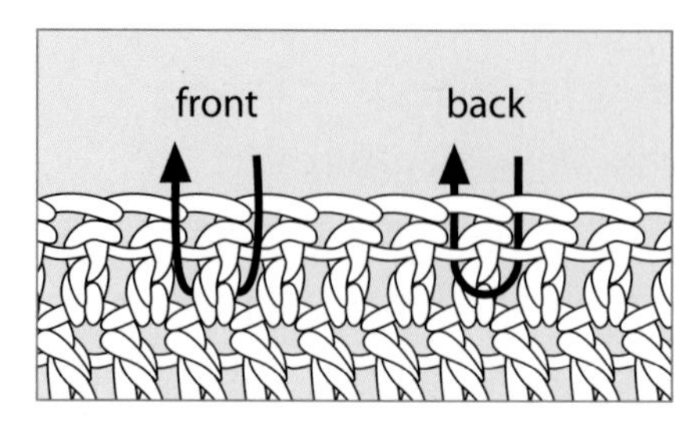

WHIPSTITCH

With **wrong** sides together, matching stitches, sew through both pieces once to secure the beginning of the seam, leaving an ample yarn end to weave in later. Insert the needle from **front** to **back** through **both** loops on **both** pieces *(Fig. 8)*. Bring the needle around and insert it from **front** to **back** through the next loops on both pieces. Continue in this manner across, keeping the sewing yarn fairly loose.

Fig. 5

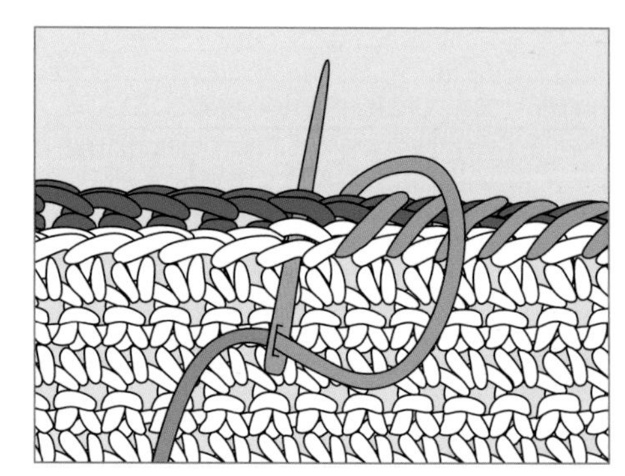

WEAVING SEAMS

With the **right** side of **both** pieces facing you and edges even, sew through both sides once to secure the seam, leaving an ample yarn end to weave in later. Insert the needle from **right** to **left** through one strand on each piece *(Fig. 6)*. Bring the needle around and insert it from **right** to **left** through the next strands on **both** pieces. Continue in this manner, drawing seam together as you work.

Fig. 6

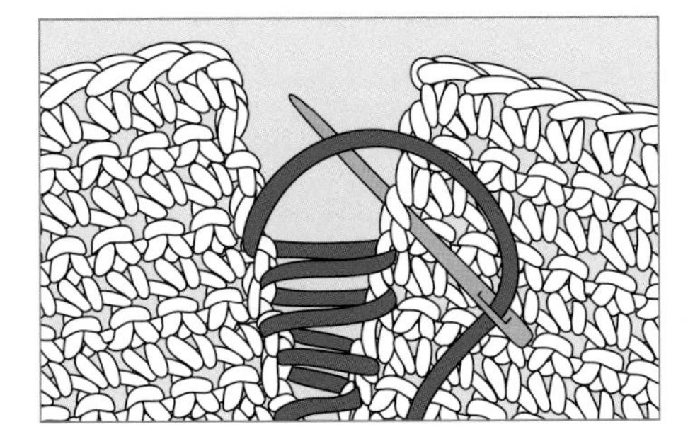

REVERSE SINGLE CROCHET

(abbreviated reverse sc)

Working from **left** to **right**, ★ insert hook in stitch to **right** of hook *(Fig. 7a)*, YO and draw through, under and to left of loop on hook (2 loops on hook) *(Fig. 7b)*, YO and draw through both loops on hook *(Fig. 7c)* (reverse sc made, *Fig. 7d)*; repeat from ★ around.

Fig. 7a

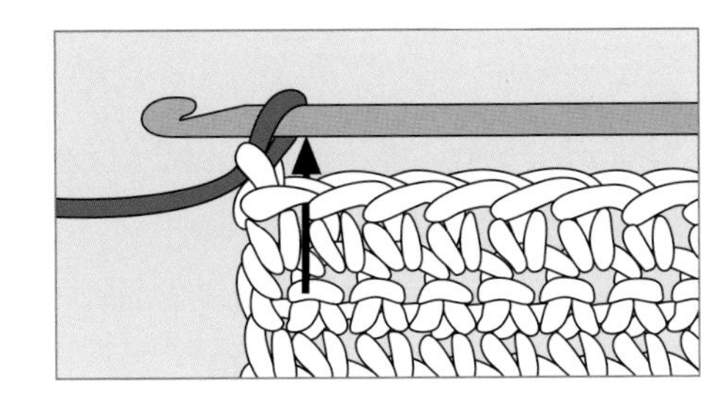

Fig. 7b

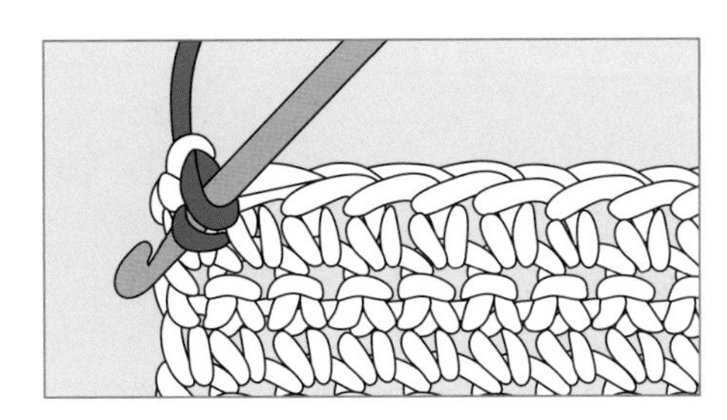

Fig. 7c

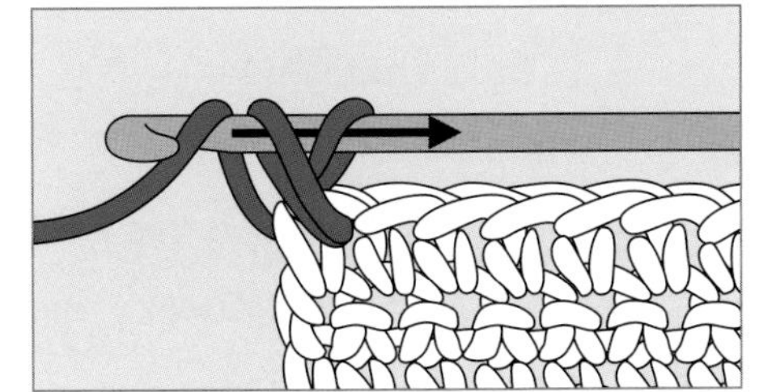

Fig. 7d

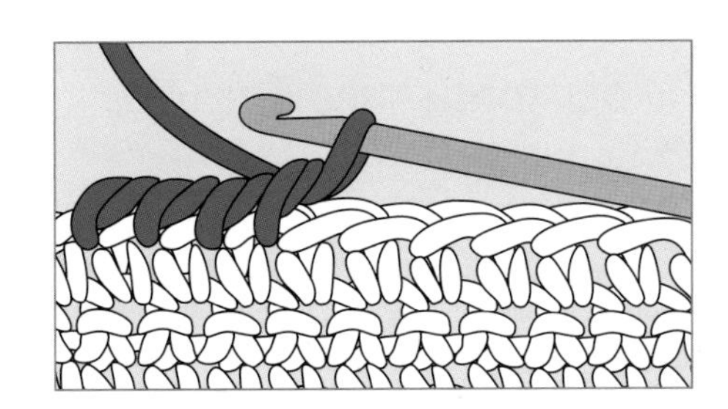

BEGINNER	Projects for first-time crocheters using basic stitches. Minimal shaping.
EASY	Projects using yarn with basic stitches, repetitive stitch patterns, simple color changes, and simple shaping and finishing.
INTERMEDIATE	Projects using a variety of techniques, such as basic lace patterns or color patterns, mid-level shaping and finishing.
EXPERIENCED	Projects with intricate stitch patterns, techniques and dimension, such as non-repeating patterns, multi-color techniques, fine threads, small hooks, detailed shaping and refined finishing.

CROCHET HOOKS																		
U.S.	B-1	C-2	D-3	E-4	F-5	G-6	7	H-8	I-9	J-10	K-10½	L-11	M/N-13	N/P-15	P/Q	Q	S
Metric - mm	2.25	2.75	3.25	3.5	3.75	4	4.5	5	5.5	6	6.5	8	9	10	15	16	19

Yarn Information

The projects in this book were made using Medium Weight yarn. Any brand of Medium Weight yarn may be used. It is best to refer to the yardage/meters when determining how many balls or skeins to purchase. Remember, to arrive at the finished size, it is the GAUGE/TENSION that is important, not the brand of yarn.

For your convenience, listed below are the specific yarns used to create our photography models.

ROPE CABLE INFINITY COWL
Patons® Decor
#87521 Frond

SEXTON BRAID HAT
Caron® Simply Soft®
#0008 Autumn Maize

HEIRLOOM ARAN AFGHAN
Lion Brand® Vanna's Choice®
#130 Honey

DIAMONDS THROW PILLOW
Caron® Simply Soft®
#9702 Off White

BALLYKEERAN FINGERLESS MITTS
Patons® Classic Wool Worsted™
#77412 Natural Heather

INNISBERRY PULLOVER
Patons® Classic Wool Worsted™
#77710 Cherry